Fiscal Year 2012
REPORT TO THE CONGRESS

U.S. GOVERNMENT
RECEIVABLES AND DEBT COLLECTION
ACTIVITIES OF FEDERAL AGENCIES

Department of the Treasury
March 2013

I0448557

DEPARTMENT OF THE TREASURY
WASHINGTON, DC

OFFICE OF THE FISCAL ASSISTANT SECRETARY

A MESSAGE FROM THE FISCAL ASSISTANT SECRETARY

I am pleased to present the *Fiscal Year 2012 Report to the Congress on U.S. Government Receivables and Debt Collection Activities of Federal Agencies*. This annual report provides important information to the American public on the status and collection of the Federal government's non-tax receivables and delinquent debt.

At the end of Fiscal Year (FY) 2012, outstanding non-tax receivables owed to the United States totaled $931.1 billion, an increase of $153.3 billion from FY 2011. These receivables represent loans to students, small business owners, homeowners, farmers, and veterans. They also represent administrative non-tax receivables, including fines and penalties, overpayments, and fees.

Most citizens pay their debt on time. However, at the end of FY 2012, delinquent non-tax debt owed to the Federal government rose to $162.7 billion, an increase of $31.7 billion over the prior fiscal year. The timely and efficient collection of delinquent debts helps fund government operations, maintain key programs and reduce the Federal deficit. Thus, it is more important than ever to continue to find ways to cost-effectively collect the past-due debt owed to the government, while, at the same time, providing debtors with due process and the opportunity to repay debt in accordance with their financial ability to pay.

The Debt Collection Improvement Act of 1996 centralized administrative delinquent debt collection functions at the Department of the Treasury (Treasury). Since implementation, Treasury's Bureau of the Fiscal Service has collected more than $62.0 billion for Federal and State agencies, including State child support agencies. In FY 2012, the Bureau of the Fiscal Service collected a record $6.2 billion at a relatively small cost to the Federal government – $49.00 are collected for every $1 spent. Despite these successes, we can do more to increase debt collection and reduce the cost of collection. In times of reduced agency budgets, it is more critical than ever to prioritize and centralize the collection of the Federal government's receivables so that limited resources may be allocated to meet the important needs of our citizens.

Richard L. Gregg

CONTENTS

I. OVERVIEW

The Secretary of the Treasury (Secretary) reports to Congress annually on the Federal government's outstanding non-tax receivables and debt collection activities. As required by Federal law (31 U.S.C. § 3719), this report includes information that Federal creditor agencies provide to the Secretary on the status of their accounts receivable and delinquent debt, as reported on the Treasury Report on Receivables and Debt Collection Activities (TROR). For more information about the TROR, visit *http://fms.treas.gov/debt/dmrpts.html*.

In furtherance of the policies promulgated by Congress and the President, Federal creditor agencies make loans directly to borrowers, guarantee loans made by private lending institutions, and impose fines and penalties. This activity results in the creation of accounts receivable as assets of the government. In addition, Federal creditor agencies award grants and make payments, which, in certain circumstances, can also result in the creation of accounts receivable.

In Fiscal Year (FY) 2012, the government's outstanding non-tax receivables totaled $931.1 billion, an increase of $153.3 billion (19.7 percent) from FY 2011. When the government's receivables are not paid by the applicable due date or in the appropriate manner, they become delinquent debt. In FY 2012, delinquent non-tax debt owed to the United States totaled $162.7 billion, an increase of $31.7 billion (24.2 percent) from FY 2011.

Each Federal creditor agency is required to make every reasonable effort to collect its delinquent debt, using collection tools described in this report. The Department of the Treasury (Treasury) and the Department of Justice (DOJ) share responsibility for setting government-wide policy on delinquent non-tax debt collection, and each plays a major role in the centralized collection of delinquent non-tax debt. In FY 2012, Federal creditor agencies collected $26.7 billion of delinquent non-tax debt, an increase of $8.4 billion (46.1 percent) from FY 2011.

- *Treasury's Bureau of the Fiscal Service* collected $2.4 billion in delinquent Federal non-tax debt in FY 2012, a 6.0 percent decrease from FY 2011. The Bureau of the Fiscal Service collects debt on behalf of Federal creditor agencies through its Cross-Servicing Program using a variety of debt collection tools. The Bureau of the Fiscal Service also collects debt on behalf of Federal creditor agencies through its Treasury Offset Program (TOP), by intercepting Federal and State payments. The Bureau of the Fiscal Service also collects delinquent Federal tax debt and delinquent debt owed to State agencies (see Appendix IV). Since 1996, The Bureau of the Fiscal Service has recovered a total of more than $62.0 billion on behalf of Federal and State agencies, including $25.6 billion in delinquent Federal non-tax debt, $3.9 billion in delinquent Federal tax debt, and $32.4 billion in delinquent debt owed to State agencies, which includes $28.2 billion in delinquent child support obligations.

- *The Department of Justice (DOJ)* collected $6.5 billion in FY 2012 in delinquent non-tax debt owed to Federal creditor agencies through its civil collection program, a 32.7 percent increase from FY 2011. DOJ has collected a total of $21.9 billion through civil litigation cash collection over the last five fiscal years.

Note: Delinquencies and collections result from various events and conditions that can occur over multiple reporting periods. Therefore, caution must be exercised when comparing annual totals and year-over-year changes of receivables, delinquencies, and collections. Depending on the structure of repayment terms, for example, the date that a receivable is due may be in the same fiscal year that it is booked or it may be in a future fiscal year. Similarly, collections during FY 2012 may be associated with non-tax debt that became delinquent either in FY 2012 or in a prior year, and are most often associated with receivables that were booked in a prior fiscal year.

II. NON-TAX RECEIVABLES OWED TO THE UNITED STATES

A. TOTAL NON-TAX RECEIVABLES

Federal non-tax receivables are amounts owed to the Federal government by a person (including individuals, organizations, and other entities). Receivables are categorized as being current or delinquent.

At the end of FY 2012, total outstanding non-tax receivables owed to the United States totaled $931.1 billion, an increase of $153.3 billion (19.7 percent) from FY 2011. The total outstanding receivable balance at the end of a fiscal year is the net of new receivables booked during that fiscal year, plus receivables owed from prior years (that have not been collected or written off) less collections, adjustments, and amounts written off.

New non-tax receivables booked during FY 2012 totaled $369.4 billion, a decrease of $10.0 billion (2.6 percent) from FY 2011. Collection on non-tax receivables was $239.9 billion, a decrease of $5.4 billion (2.2 percent) from FY 2011.

FIGURE 1

OUTSTANDING FEDERAL NON-TAX RECEIVABLES AS OF SEPTEMBER 30: FY 2008-2012
(DOLLARS IN BILLIONS)

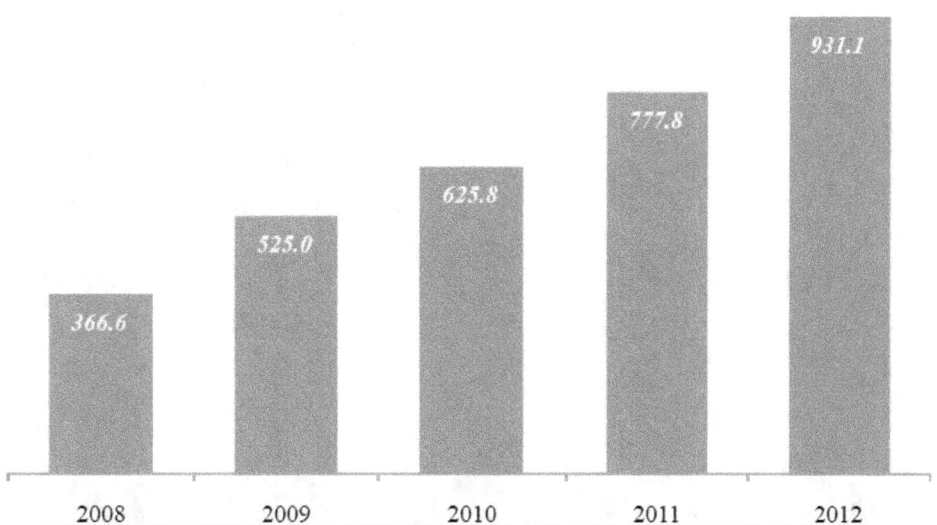

SOURCE: TREASURY REPORT ON RECEIVABLES AND DEBT COLLECTION ACTIVITIES – FOURTH QUARTER FY 2008 - 2012

FIGURE 2

NEW FEDERAL NON-TAX RECEIVABLES, BY FISCAL YEAR BOOKED: FY 2008-2012
(DOLLARS IN BILLIONS)

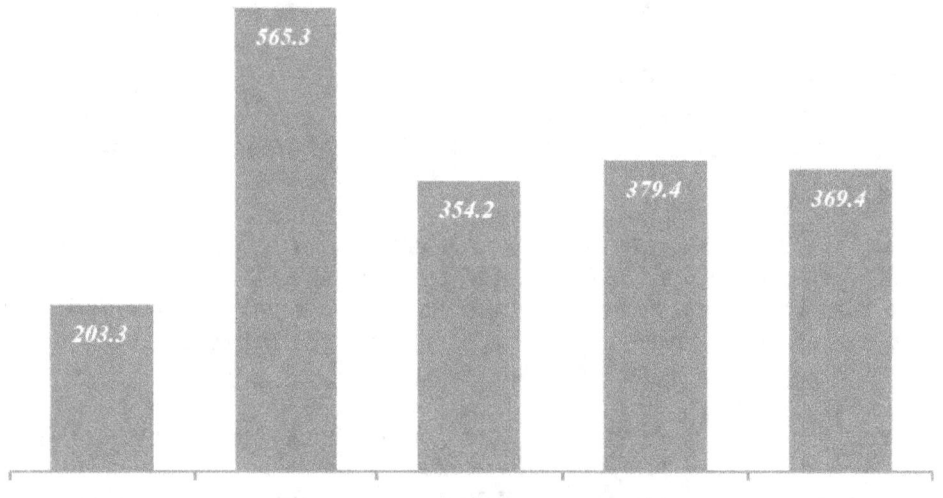

SOURCE: TREASURY REPORT ON RECEIVABLES AND DEBT COLLECTION ACTIVITIES –
FOURTH QUARTER FY 2008 - 2012

FIGURE 3

TOTAL COLLECTION ON FEDERAL NON-TAX RECEIVABLES: FY 2008-2012
(DOLLARS IN BILLIONS)

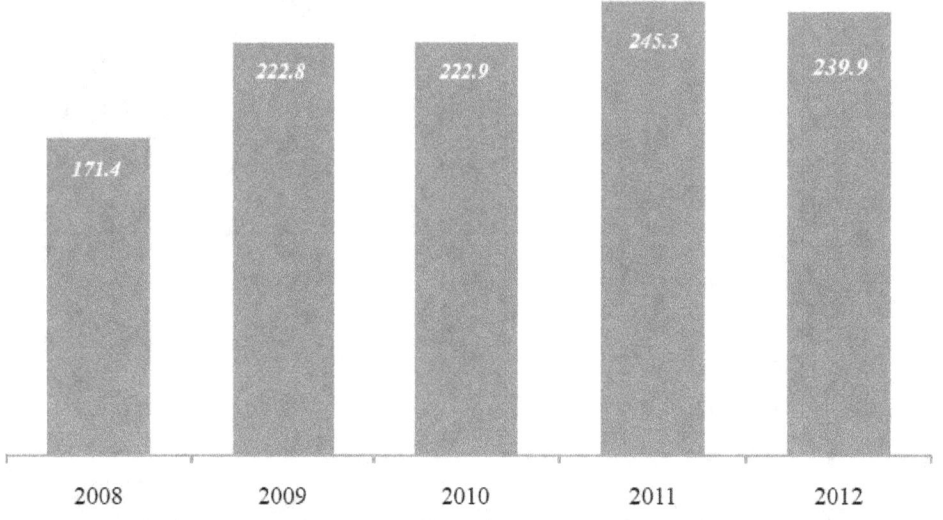

SOURCE: TREASURY REPORT ON RECEIVABLES AND DEBT COLLECTION ACTIVITIES –
FOURTH QUARTER FY 2008 - 2012

FIGURE 4

YEAR-TO-YEAR CHANGE IN COLLECTION OF FEDERAL NON-TAX RECEIVABLES:
TOP FIVE CREDITOR AGENCIES

AGENCY	FY 2012 (Billions)	CHANGE FROM FY 2011
Education	$59.9	-3.9%
HHS	$42.4	7.5%
USDA	$25.9	7.7%
DoD	$15.7	60.7%
HUD	$13.4	14.9%
All Others	$82.6	-17.7%
TOTAL GOVERNMENT	**$239.9**	**-2.2%**

SOURCE: TREASURY REPORT ON RECEIVABLES AND DEBT COLLECTION ACTIVITIES –
FOURTH QUARTER FY 2012

1. BY CREDITOR AGENCY

Together, the Department of Education (Education) and the Department of Agriculture (USDA) account for $762.1 billion (81.9 percent) of the government's total outstanding receivables.

- **Education**: In FY 2012, Education collected $59.9 billion in non-tax receivables, a decrease of $2.4 billion (3.9 percent) from FY 2011, including loan consolidations. At the end of FY 2012, Education's outstanding receivables totaled $643.3 billion, 69.1 percent of the government's total receivables. Federal Direct Student Loans ($596.0 billion) and Defaulted Guaranteed Student Loans ($47.0 billion) account for more than 99 percent of Education's total receivables.

- **USDA:** In FY 2012, non-tax receivables collection for USDA totaled $25.9 billion, an increase of $1.9 billion (7.7 percent) from FY 2011. At the end of FY 2012, USDA's outstanding receivables totaled $118.8 billion, 12.8 percent of the government's total receivables. The Rural Development Fund ($94.0 billion), Commodity Credit Corporation ($10.1 billion), Farm Service Agency ($8.5 billion), Federal Crop Insurance ($5.3 billion), and Food and Nutrition Service ($0.4 billion) account for more than 99 percent of USDA's total receivables.

FIGURE 5

YEAR-TO-YEAR CHANGE IN OUTSTANDING FEDERAL NON-TAX RECEIVABLES:
TOP FIVE CREDITOR AGENCIES

AGENCY	FY 2012 (Billions)	CHANGE FROM FY 2011
Education	$643.3	27.5%
USDA	$118.8	2.3%
Treasury	$23.1	6.7%
HUD	$20.8	9.2%
SSA	$16.6	4.3%
All Others	$108.5	8.1%
TOTAL GOVERNMENT	**$931.1**	**19.7%**

SOURCE: TREASURY REPORT ON RECEIVABLES AND DEBT COLLECTION ACTIVITIES –
FOURTH QUARTER FY 2012

FIGURE 6

OUTSTANDING FEDERAL NON-TAX RECEIVABLES AS OF SEPTEMBER 30, 2012:
TOP FIVE CREDITOR AGENCIES

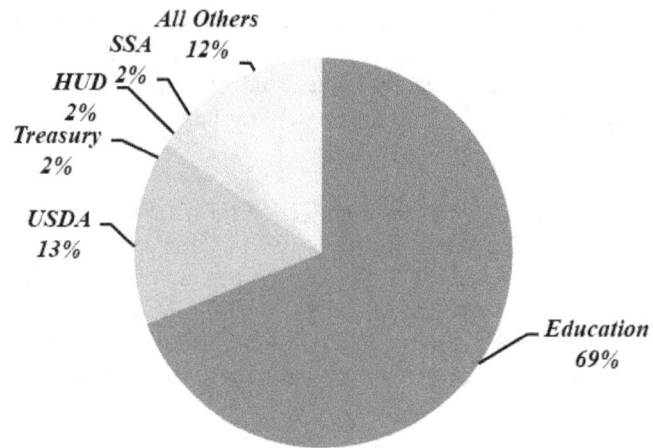

SOURCE: TREASURY REPORT ON RECEIVABLES AND DEBT COLLECTION ACTIVITIES –
FOURTH QUARTER FY 2012

2. BY RECEIVABLE TYPE

Of the $931.1 billion in Federal non-tax receivables outstanding at the end of FY 2012, Federal loan receivables (direct and defaulted guaranteed loans) represented $844.5 billion (90.7 percent), an increase of $150.8 billion (21.7 percent) from FY 2011. Administrative receivables (all non-loan receivables[1]) represented $86.6 billion (9.3 percent) of the total outstanding receivables in FY 2012, an increase of $2.5 billion (3.0 percent) from FY 2011.

FIGURE 7

OUTSTANDING FEDERAL NON-TAX RECEIVABLES AS OF SEPTEMBER 30, BY TYPE: FY 2008-2012
(DOLLARS IN BILLIONS)

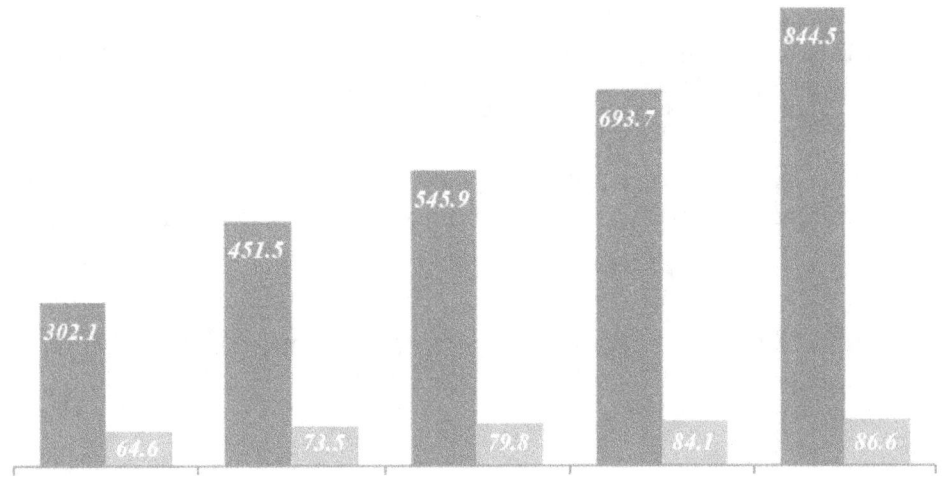

■ *Loans (Direct and Guaranteed)*   ■ *Administrative (Non-Loan)*

SOURCE: TREASURY REPORT ON RECEIVABLES AND DEBT COLLECTION ACTIVITIES –
FOURTH QUARTER FY 2008 - 2012

B. INTEREST, PENALTIES, AND ADMINISTRATIVE COSTS

Generally, Federal creditor agencies apply interest on outstanding loan receivables and apply penalties and administrative costs when the receivables become delinquent. Of the $931.1 billion in outstanding receivables at the end of FY 2012, $58.3 billion (6.3 percent) represented unpaid interest, penalties, and administrative costs.

---

[1] Non-loan receivables include fines, penalties, and overpayments.

III. DELINQUENT NON-TAX DEBT OWED TO THE UNITED STATES

A. TOTAL DELINQUENT NON-TAX DEBT

A non-tax debt is considered delinquent if it has not been paid by the date specified in an agency's initial written demand for payment or applicable agreement. A non-tax debt may become delinquent during the same fiscal year that it was booked as a receivable or during a subsequent fiscal year.

At the end of FY 2012, outstanding delinquent non-tax debt owed to the United States totaled $162.7 billion, an increase of $31.7 billion (24.2 percent) from FY 2011. The total outstanding delinquent debt balance at the end of a fiscal year is the net of debt that remained delinquent from previous fiscal years and debt that became delinquent during that fiscal year less collections, adjustments, and amounts written off.

Of the $162.7 billion in outstanding delinquent debt as of the end of FY 2012, a total of $96.7 billion became delinquent during FY 2012,[2] an increase of $27.2 billion (39.1 percent) from FY 2011.

FIGURE 8

FEDERAL DELINQUENT NON-TAX DEBT AS OF SEPTEMBER 30: FY 2008-2012
(DOLLARS IN BILLIONS)

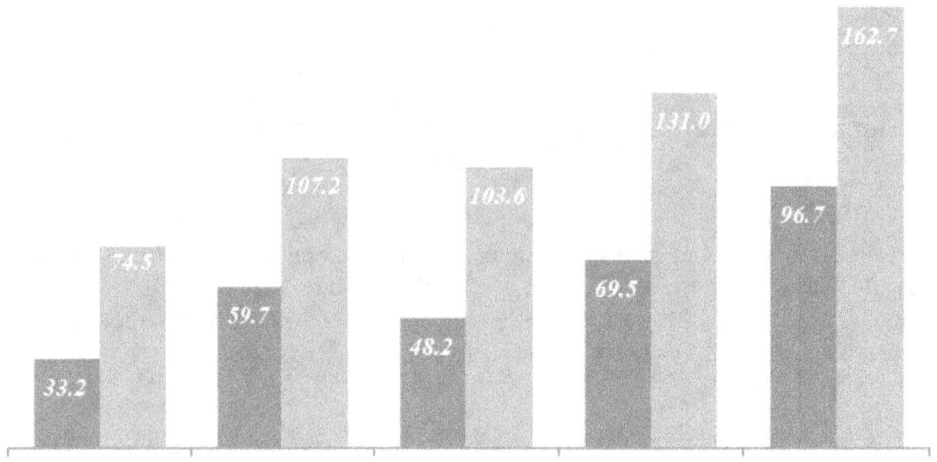

Outstanding Debt <365 Days Delinquent   *Total Outstanding Debt*

SOURCE: TREASURY REPORT ON RECEIVABLES AND DEBT COLLECTION ACTIVITIES –
FOURTH QUARTER FY 2008 - 2012

---

[2] Debt that was between 1 and 365 days delinquent as of September 30, 2012.

1. BY AGE

Of the $162.7 billion in delinquent Federal non-tax debt, $116.2 billion (71.4 percent) is less than two years delinquent. Generally, Federal creditor agencies are required to write off delinquent non-tax debt older than two years. At the end of FY 2012, 28.6 percent of outstanding delinquent non-tax debt was more than two years old, down from 33.2 percent in FY 2011.

FIGURE 9

TOTAL FEDERAL NON-TAX DELINQUENCIES, BY AGE: FY 2012

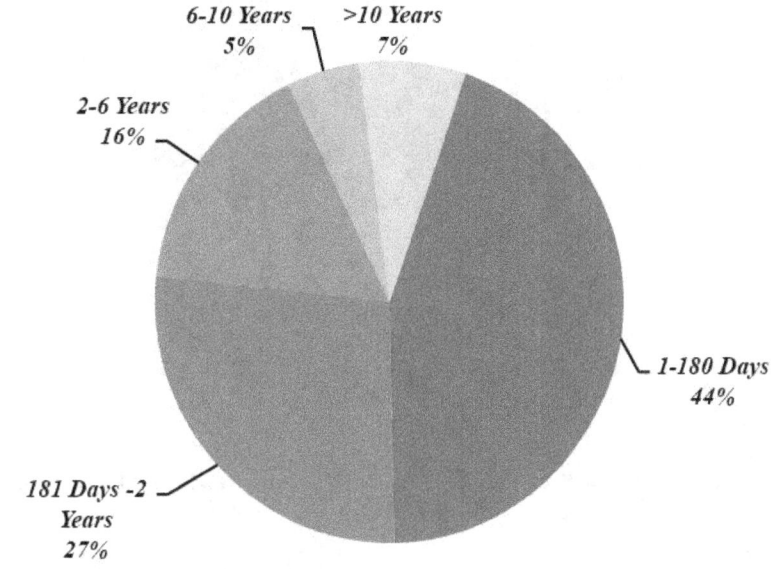

SOURCE: TREASURY REPORT ON RECEIVABLES AND DEBT COLLECTION ACTIVITIES –
FOURTH QUARTER FY 2012

FIGURE 10

FEDERAL NON-TAX DELINQUENCIES, BY AGE: FY 2008 – E NEN
(DOLLARS IN BILLIONS)

DELINQUENCY AGE	FY 2008	FY 2009	FY2010	FY 2011	FY 2012
1-180 Days	$21.1	$48.9	$34.3	$49.7	$72.2
181 Days-2 Years	$23.2	$24.1	$29.7	$37.7	$44.0
2-6 Years	$12.7	$20.5	$22.9	$26.5	$26.4
6-10 Years	$6.1	$4.5	$5.4	$5.2	$8.2
> 10 Years	$11.4	$9.2	$11.3	$11.9	$11.9
TOTAL	**$74.5**	**$107.2**	**$103.6**	**$131.0**	**$162.7**

SOURCE: TREASURY REPORT ON RECEIVABLES AND DEBT COLLECTION ACTIVITIES –
FOURTH QUARTER FY 2008 – 2012

12

2. BY CREDITOR AGENCY

By the close of FY 2012, $144.7 billion (89.0 percent) delinquent debt owed to five Federal creditor agencies: Education, Department of Housing and Urban Development (HUD), Small Business Administration (SBA), DoD, and SSA.

FIGURE 11

FEDERAL NON-TAX DELINQUENCIES IN FY 2012: TOP FIVE CREDITOR AGENCIES

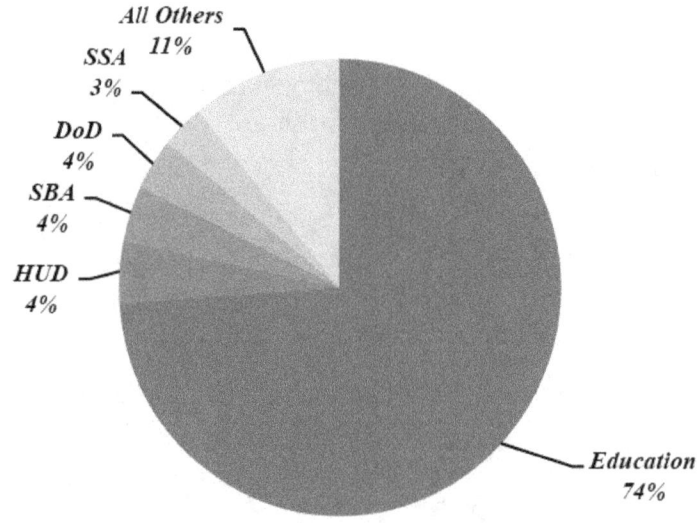

SOURCE: TREASURY REPORT ON RECEIVABLES AND DEBT COLLECTION ACTIVITIES –
FOURTH QUARTER FY 2012

FIGURE 12

YEAR-TO-YEAR CHANGE IN FEDERAL NON-TAX DELINQUENCIES:
TOP FIVE CREDITOR AGENCIES

AGENCY	FY 2012 (Billions)	CHANGE FROM FY 2011
Education	$120.2	30.5%
HUD	$7.2	9.0%
SBA	$6.5	16.1%
DoD	$5.9	11.0%
SSA	$5.0	7.2%
All Others	$17.9	6.8%
TOTAL GOVERNMENT	*$162.7*	*24.2%*

SOURCE: TREASURY REPORT ON RECEIVABLES AND DEBT COLLECTION ACTIVITIES –
FOURTH QUARTER FY 2012

3. BY DEBT TYPE

Federal loan program delinquencies comprised $134.5 billion (82.7 percent) of total delinquencies at the end of FY 2012, up slightly from 81.9 percent in FY 2011. Administrative delinquencies for FY 2012 totaled $28.2 billion, an increase of $4.5 billion (18.9 percent) from FY 2011.

FIGURE 13

FEDERAL NON-TAX DELINQUENT DEBT, BY TYPE: FY 2008-2012
(DOLLARS IN BILLIONS)

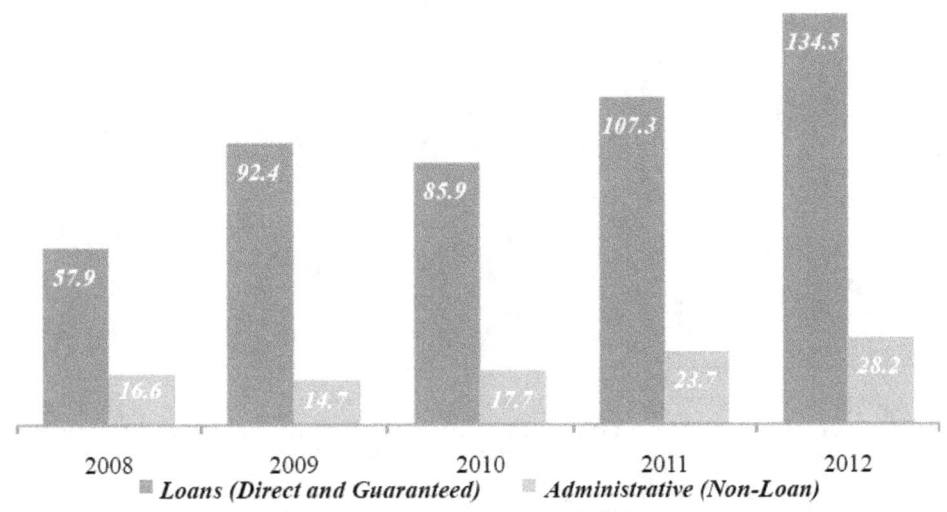

SOURCE: TREASURY REPORT ON RECEIVABLES AND DEBT COLLECTION ACTIVITIES –
FOURTH QUARTER FY 2008 - 2012

IV. DELINQUENT NON-TAX DEBT COLLECTION ACTIVITIES

A. TOTAL DELINQUENT NON-TAX DEBT COLLECTION

In FY 2012, Federal creditor agencies collected $26.7 billion in delinquent non-tax debt. Delinquent non-tax debt collection increased by $8.4 billion (46.1 percent) from FY 2011.

FIGURE 14

COLLECTION ON DELINQUENT NON-TAX DEBT: FY 2008-2012
(DOLLARS IN BILLIONS)

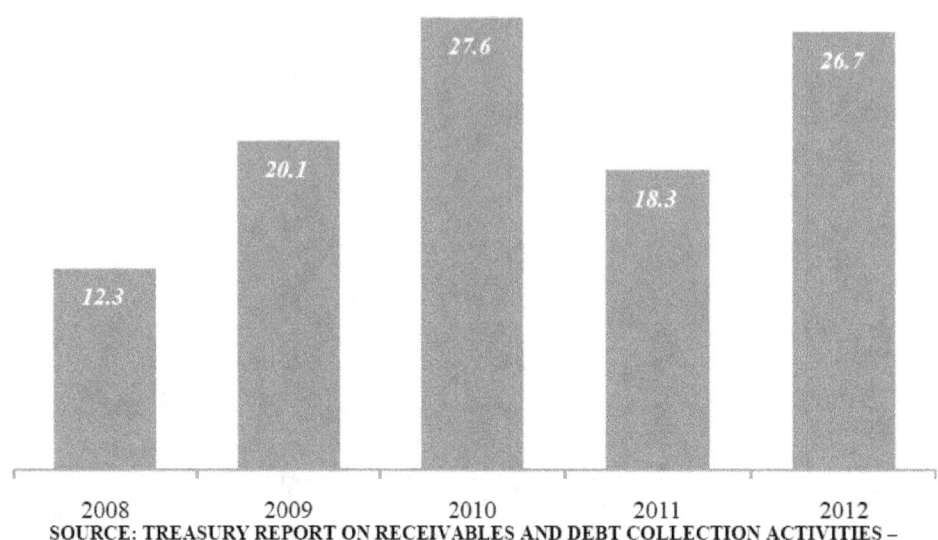

**SOURCE: TREASURY REPORT ON RECEIVABLES AND DEBT COLLECTION ACTIVITIES –
FOURTH QUARTER FY 2008 - 2012**

1. BY CREDITOR AGENCY

More than $21.0 billion (79.5 percent) of the delinquent non-tax debt collected in FY 2012 was owed to five Federal creditor agencies: Education (37.4 percent), HUD (19.5 percent), Department of Health and Human Services (HHS) (9.4 percent), Department of Homeland Security (DHS) (9.0 percent), and USDA (4.5 percent).

FIGURE 15

YEAR-TO-YEAR CHANGE IN COLLECTION OF FEDERAL NON-TAX DELINQUENCIES: TOP FIVE CREDITOR AGENCIES

AGENCY	FY 2012 (Billions)	CHANGE FROM FY 2011
Education	$10.0	34.3%
HUD	$5.2	75.7%
HHS	$2.5	110.5%
DHS	$2.4	608.3%
USDA	$1.2	13.6%
All Others	$5.4	1.2%
TOTAL GOVERNMENT	$26.7	46.1%

SOURCE: TREASURY REPORT ON RECEIVABLES AND DEBT COLLECTION ACTIVITIES – FOURTH QUARTER FY 2012

FIGURE 16

COLLECTION OF FEDERAL NON-TAX DELINQUENT DEBT IN FY 2012: TOP FIVE CREDITOR AGENCIES

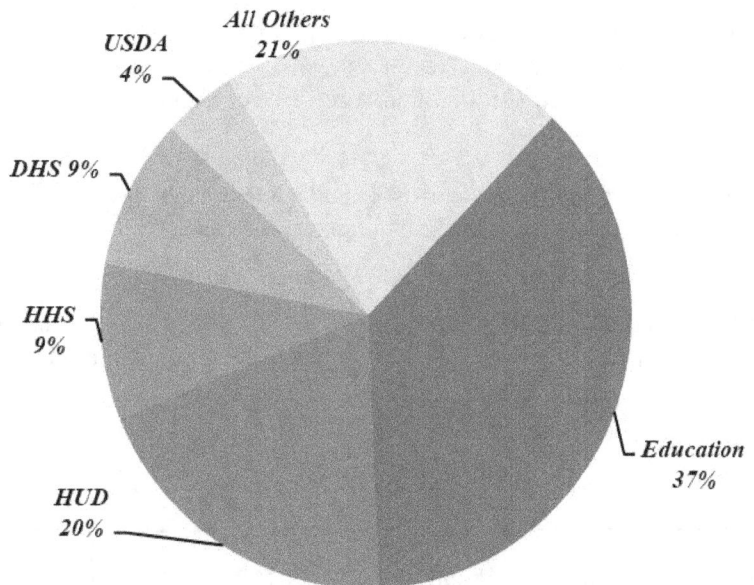

SOURCE: TREASURY REPORT ON RECEIVABLES AND DEBT COLLECTION ACTIVITIES FOURTH QUARTER FY 2012

2. BY COLLECTION TOOL

Federal creditor agencies use a variety of tools to collect delinquent Federal non-tax debt. Collection tools include garnishment of wages, use of private collection agencies (PCAs), offset of Federal and State payments, and litigation. The use of administrative wage garnishment (AWG) and PCAs is discussed below.

A. AWG Collection

Federal creditor agencies are authorized to garnish a delinquent debtor's non-Federal wages without obtaining a court order (31 U.S.C. § 3720D). This process is known as "administrative wage garnishment." PCAs may assist Treasury and other Federal creditor agencies in the initiation of an AWG. The goal of AWG is to ensure that every employed debtor is repaying his or her debt owed to the United States. Before issuing an AWG order, Federal creditor agencies must first provide a debtor with notice and an opportunity to enter into a repayment agreement, dispute the debt, or object to the intended garnishment action. In FY 2012, Federal creditor agencies collected $796.5 million through the use of AWG, an increase of $500.6 million (169.1 percent).

B. PCA Collection

Federal creditor agencies are authorized to contract with PCAs to collect delinquent non-tax debt owed to the United States (31 U.S.C. § 3718). PCAs assist Federal creditor agencies in many ways, including locating debtors, establishing repayment agreements and resolving debt administratively when a debtor is deceased, unable to pay, disabled, bankrupt, or out of business.

- **Treasury** contracts with PCAs to collect delinquent non-tax debt referred by Federal creditor agencies participating in Treasury's Cross-Servicing Program. In FY 2012, Treasury's PCAs collected $81.4 million, a decrease of $6.5 million (7.4 percent) from FY 2011.

- **Education** contracts with PCAs to assist in collecting defaulted student loan debt. In FY 2012, Education's PCAs collected $2.9 billion, an increase of $300.0 million (11.3 percent) from FY 2011.

- **HHS**'s Program Support Center (PSC) contracts with a PCA to collect delinquent debt. In FY 2012, PSC's PCA collected $1.7 million, a decrease of $1.2 million (41.4 percent) from FY 2011.

FIGURE 17

COLLECTION BY PCAs: FY 2008-2012
(DOLLARS IN MILLIONS)

CREDITOR AGENCY	FY 2008	FY 2009	FY 2010	FY 2011	FY 2012
HHS	$3.8	$2.2	$1.7	$2.9	$1.7
Treasury[1]	$82.8	$132.1	$90.3	$87.9	$81.4
Education[1,2]	$2,291.0	$2,416.0	$2,354.0	$2,644.0	$2,944.0

[1]Includes collection by administrative wage garnishment.
[2]Includess loan consolidation and rehabilitations.

SOURCES: DEPARTMENT OF HEALTH AND HUMAN SERVICES, PROGRAM SUPPORT CENTER
            DEPARTMENT OF THE TREASURY, BUREAU OF THE FISCAL SERVICE
            DEPARTMENT OF EDUCATION, DEFAULT RESOLUTION GROUP

B. DEPARTMENT OF THE TREASURY'S DEBT COLLECTION PROGRAMS

Generally, Federal creditor agencies are required to refer non-tax debt that are 180 days delinquent to Treasury for collection through its TOP and its Cross-Servicing Program. For non-tax debt submitted to TOP, Treasury intercepts eligible Federal and State payments and applies them to a payee's delinquent non-tax debt. For non-tax debt submitted to the Cross-Servicing Program, Treasury contacts debtors by demand letters and telephone calls, negotiates payment agreements, submits debt to TOP, refers debt to private collection agencies and DOJ, reports debt to credit bureaus, and initiates administrative wage garnishment. Before submitting a non-tax debt to Treasury, Federal creditor agencies must send the debtor a notice describing the debt, the collection actions to be taken, and the opportunities available to the debtor to repay or challenge the debt.

Certain types of non-tax debt are ineligible for referral to TOP or Cross-Servicing, including non-tax debt that are the subject of an appeal, forbearance agreement, litigation, foreclosure, or bankruptcy. Certain other non-tax debt are eligible for TOP and Cross-Servicing, but are exempt from the general mandatory requirement that they be referred to Cross-Servicing, including debt being serviced by a PCA, debt being collected by internal offset or administrative wage garnishment, and Treasury-exempted debt.

1. TREASURY'S OFFSET PROGRAM

In FY 2012, Treasury collected $6.0 billion through TOP, a decrease of $12.0 million (0.2 percent) from FY 2011. This number includes TOP collection on delinquent Federal non-tax debt ($2.4 billion), as well as collection on delinquent Federal tax debt ($601.6 million)[3] and debt owed to State agencies ($3.0 billion), including delinquent child support obligations. See Appendix IV for more information.

TOP eligible payments include Federal tax refunds, Social Security, retirement, salary, vendor, and other Federal payments, as well as State tax refunds and other payments made by several States participating in TOP.[4]

FIGURE 19

TOP COLLECTION OF FEDERAL NON-TAX DEBT BY PAYMENT TYPE: FY 2008-2012
(DOLLARS IN MILLIONS)

PAYMENT TYPE	FY 2008	FY 2009	FY 2010	FY 2011	FY 2012
Federal Tax Refund Payment	*$1,948.0*	*$1,400.0*	*$1,852.0*	*$2,180.0*	*$2,018.9*
Federal Non-Tax Payment	*$216.2*	*$511.9*	*$313.0*	*$390.0*	*$399.1*
TOTAL	*$2,164.2*	*$1,911.9*	*$2,165.0*	*$2,570.0*	*$2,418.0*

SOURCE: DEPARTMENT OF THE TREASURY, BUREAU OF THE FISCAL SERVICE

---

[3] The Bureau of the Fiscal Service assists the Internal Revenue Service with the collection of Federal tax debt through TOP.

[4] Generally, one-time payments (tax refunds and vendor payments) may be offset up to 100% of the payment amount. For recurring payments (Social Security, retirement, and salary), the offset amount is limited to a percentage of the payment.

18

2. TREASURY'S CROSS-SERVICING PROGRAM

In FY 2012, Treasury collected $262.9 million through its Cross-Servicing Program, an increase of $31.7 million (13.7 percent).[5] Of that amount, $71.9 million, an increase of $22.2 million (44.7 percent) was recovered by employees of Debt Management Services (DMS), an area within Treasury's Bureau of the Fiscal Service, $81.4 million, a decrease of $6.5 million (7.4 percent) was collected by Treasury's PCAs, $108.7 million, an increase of $15.6 million (16.8 percent) was collected through TOP, and $862,000, an increase of $317,600 (58.3 percent) was collected by DOJ.

FIGURE 18

CROSS-SERVICING COLLECTIONS: FY 2008-2012
(DOLLARS IN MILLIONS)

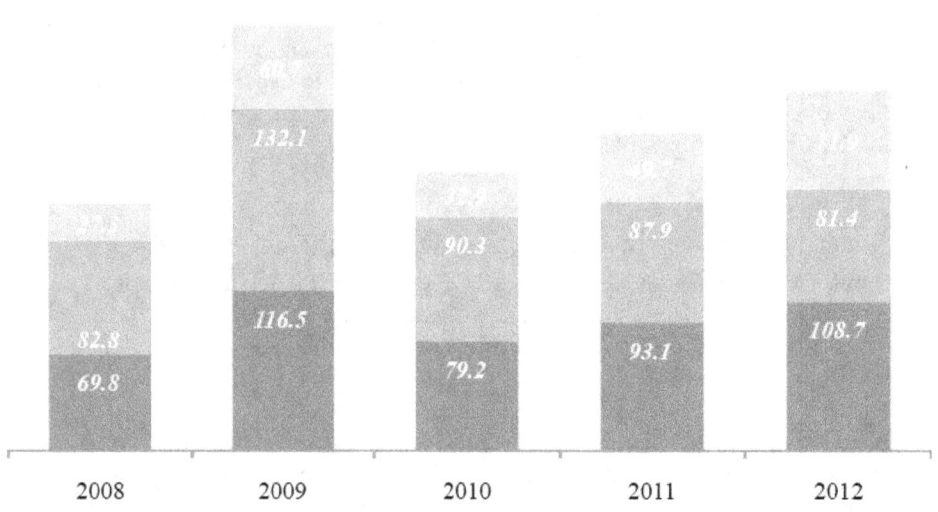

TOP *PCA* *DMS*

SOURCE: DEPARTMENT OF THE TREASURY, BUREAU OF THE FISCAL SERVICE

---

[5] Collection for non-tax debt referred to TOP through the Cross-Servicing Program are included in both the TOP and Cross-Servicing collection totals.

C. ENFORCED NON-TAX DEBT COLLECTION BY THE DEPARTMENT OF JUSTICE

When a Federal creditor agency cannot collect a non-tax debt administratively, the agency may refer the debt to DOJ to pursue enforced collection[6] through the courts. In FY 2012, Federal creditor agencies referred 7,109 cases totaling $13.1 billion to DOJ for enforced collection. In FY 2012, DOJ collected $6.5 billion[7] for Federal creditor agencies, an increase of $1.6 billion (32.6 percent) over FY 2011.

FIGURE 20

CIVIL REFERRALS TO DOJ		
FISCAL YEAR	TOTAL REFERRALS (NEW)	VALUE OF NEW DEBT (DOLLARS IN BILLIONS)
2008	*11,559*	*$3.8*
2009	*11,088*	*$5.2*
2010	*11,531*	*$7.6*
2011	*16,487*	*$6.1*
2012	*7,109*	*$13.1*

SOURCE: DEPARTMENT OF JUSTICE, OFFICE OF DEBT COLLECTION MANAGEMENT

---

[6] An "enforced" collection occurs when DOJ uses a legal process to force the involuntary payment of a debt by a debtor. Examples of enforced collection processes include a court-ordered wage garnishment sent to the debtor's employer or a bank garnishment filed with the debtor's bank, effectively seizing the funds from the debtor's pay or bank account.

[7] DOJ's collections encompass both judicial and non-judicial collection. DOJ can collect debt through non-judicial means in a number of ways: 1) payment arrangements agreed to without a court filing; 2) voluntary wage assignment prior to any proceedings in federal court; or 3) debtor's immediate payment as soon as the debtor discovers that the debt has been referred to DOJ for collection. An agency with independent litigation authority may, but is not required to, refer its debt to DOJ for litigation and collection. If an agency chooses to litigate its own debt, then DOJ has no involvement in tracking or enforcing that debt.

FIGURE 21

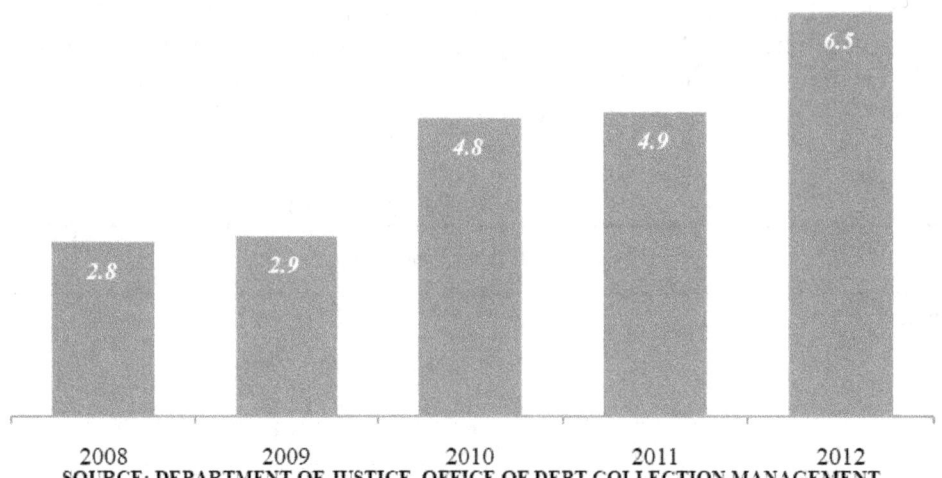

CIVIL LITIGATION CASH COLLECTION: FY 2008-2012
(DOLLARS IN BILLIONS)

SOURCE: DEPARTMENT OF JUSTICE, OFFICE OF DEBT COLLECTION MANAGEMENT

D. DEPARTMENT OF EDUCATION STUDENT LOANS[8]

Education collects delinquent student loans directly and through a network of Guaranty Agencies (GAs). Education's Default Resolution Group (DRG) services Education's defaulted student loans (loans delinquent more than 270 days) and a small number of student grant overpayments. DRG uses a variety of debt collection tools, including PCAs, AWG, and offset. Education works with the GAs to ensure that all eligible non-tax debt is certified to TOP in order to maximize the potential for collection.

In FY 2012, Education collected $13.1 billion, an increase of $1.1 billion (9.0 percent) from FY 2011.

---

[8] More information on the Education's Student Aid programs can be found in the Annual Report for Federal Student Aid (http://www2.ed.gov/about/reports/annual/index html).

FIGURE 22

ANNUAL DEPARTMENT OF EDUCATION COLLECTION: FY 2008-2012
(DOLLARS IN BILLIONS)

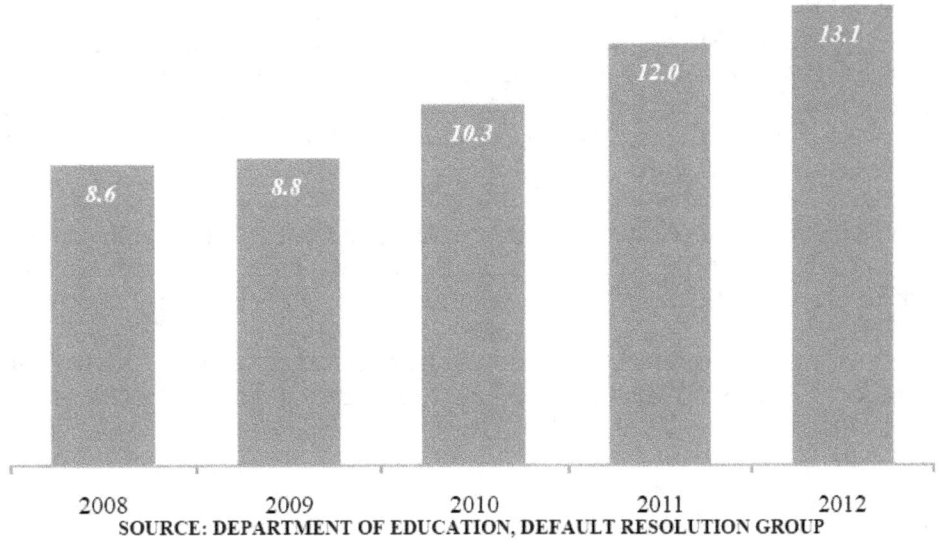

SOURCE: DEPARTMENT OF EDUCATION, DEFAULT RESOLUTION GROUP

E. DEPARTMENT OF HEALTH AND HUMAN SERVICES PROGRAM SUPPORT CENTER

In 1995, HHS established the Program Support Center (PSC), Debt Collection Center. The PSC is a Treasury-designated debt collection center that collects non-tax debt on a fee-for-service basis for 11 different Federal creditor agencies within HHS and several Federal creditor agencies outside of HHS. In addition, the PSC serves as the HHS conduit for referrals to Treasury for both TOP and Cross-Servicing. In FY 2012, the PSC collected $427.0 million, an increase of $3.3 million (0.8 percent increase) from FY 2011.

FIGURE 23

PSC COLLECTION: FY 2008-2012
(DOLLARS IN MILLIONS)

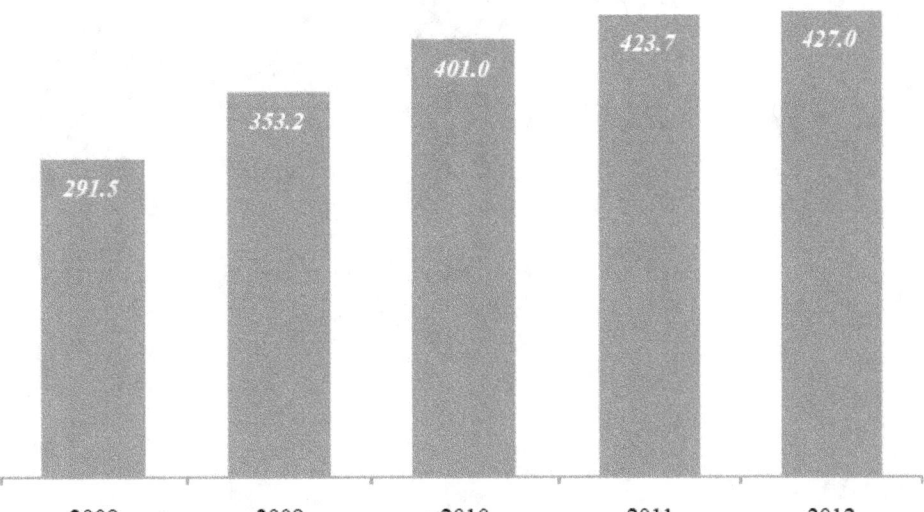

SOURCE: DEPARTMENT OF HEALTH AND HUMAN SERVICES, PROGRAM SUPPORT CENTER

V. WRITE-OFFS OF DELINQUENT NON-TAX DEBT

Federal creditor agencies are generally required to "write off" non-tax debt that is two years delinquent (see Office of Management and Budget Circular A-129). By writing off their uncollectible non-tax debt, Federal creditor agencies more accurately reflect the value of their receivables on the books of the United States. Certain write offs are categorized as "currently not collectible" (CNC), which means that collection attempts will continue until the agency decides to terminate debt collection action.

Other write-offs are categorized as "closed out," which means that a Federal creditor agency has terminated all debt collection action. Consequently, a Federal creditor agency may be required to report such write-offs to the Internal Revenue Service (IRS) as potential income to the debtor.

In FY 2012, Federal non-tax debt that was written off and closed out totaled $7.8 billion, an increase of $2.1 billion (37.9 percent) from FY 2011. The Federal creditor agencies with the largest write-off amounts in FY 2012 include Education ($4.0 billion), USDA ($1.6 billion) and SSA ($1.0 billion).

FIGURE 24

ANNUAL WRITE-OFFS: FY 2008-2012
(DOLLARS IN BILLIONS)

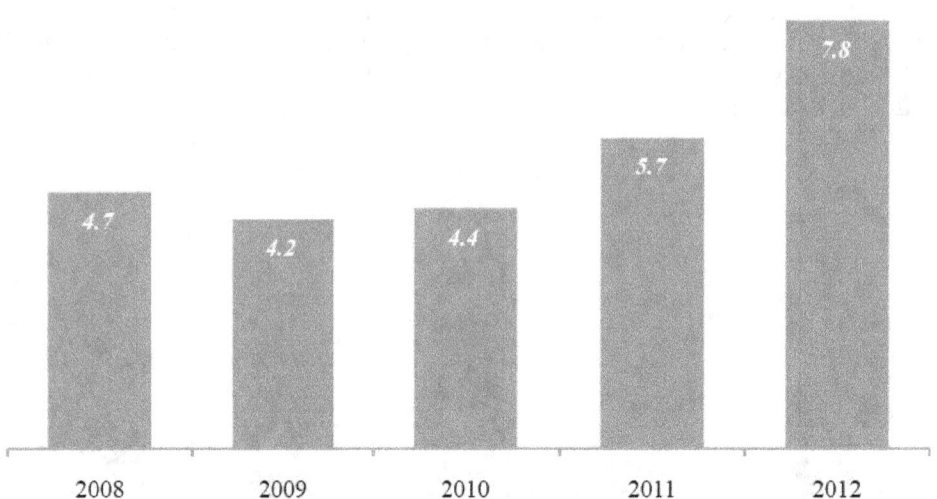

SOURCE: TREASURY REPORT ON RECEIVABLES AND DEBT COLLECTION ACTIVITIES
FOURTH QUARTER FY 2008 - 2012

APPENDIX I: TOTAL FEDERAL NON-TAX RECEIVABLES AND DELINQUENT NON-TAX DEBT BY CREDITOR AGENCY

At the end of FY 2012, 96.3 percent of Federal receivables arose from programs administered by the 10 Federal creditor agencies listed below.

FIGURE 25

TOTAL FEDERAL NON-TAX RECEIVABLES AND DELINQUENT DEBT:
TOP TEN CREDITOR AGENCIES
(DOLLARS IN MILLIONS)

AGENCY	RECEIVABLES BALANCE (AS OF SEPTEMBER 30, 2012)	DELINQUENT DEBT BALANCE (AS OF SEPTEMBER 30, 2012)
Education	$643,276.3	$120,164.2
USDA	$118,856.2	$4,586.1
Treasury	$23,067.0	$22.4
HUD	$20,792.1	$7,188.0
SSA	$16,587.7	$4,998.9
Energy	$16,235.1	$100.7
SBA	$16,140.2	$6,481.6
HHS	$14,196.4	$2,067.3
Export-Import Bank	$13,951.6	$1,588.1
DoD	$13,534.4	$5,871.2
TOP 10 TOTAL	**$896,637.0**	**$153,068.5**
ALL OTHERS	**$34,447.8**	**$9,584.9**
GOVERNMENT TOTAL	**$931,084.8**	**$162,653.4**

SOURCE: TREASURY REPORT ON RECEIVABLES AND DEBT COLLECTION ACTIVITIES –
FOURTH QUARTER FY 2008 - 2012

APPENDIX II: TOTAL FY 2012 COLLECTION OF FEDERAL DELINQUENT NON-TAX DEBT BY CREDITOR AGENCY

At the end of FY 2012, 92.2 percent of Federal collection of delinquent Federal non-tax debt was associated with debt administered by the 10 Federal creditor agencies listed below. The remaining 7.8 percent of collections arose from all other programs.

FIGURE 26

TOTAL COLLECTION OF DELINQUENT FEDERAL NON-TAX DEBT:
TOP TEN CREDITOR AGENCIES
(DOLLARS IN MILLIONS)

AGENCY	FY 2012 COLLECTIONS
Education	*$9,960.8*
HUD	*$5,221.0*
HHS	*$2,473.1*
DHS	*$2,387.5*
USDA	*$1,185.3*
DoD	*$928.4*
GSA	*$751.2*
EPA	*$637.6*
SBA	*$542.6*
Interior	*$531.9*
TOP 10 TOTAL	**$24,619.4**
ALL OTHER	**$2,071.9**
GOVERNMENT TOTAL	**$26,691.3**

SOURCE: TREASURY REPORT ON RECEIVABLES AND DEBT COLLECTION ACTIVITIES –
FOURTH QUARTER FY 2008 - 2012

APPENDIX III: TOTAL FY 2012 WRITE-OFFS BY CREDITOR AGENCY

In FY 2012, 97.3 percent of Federal debt write-offs arose from programs administered by the 10 Federal creditor agencies listed below. The remaining 2.7 percent of Federal debt write-offs arose from all other programs.

FIGURE 27

TOTAL FEDERAL WRITE-OFFS:
TOP TEN CREDITOR AGENCIES
(DOLLARS IN MILLIONS)

AGENCY	FY 2012 WRITE-OFFS
Education	$3,973.0
USDA	$1,571.6
SSA	$1,010.8
Funds Appropriated to President	$260.9
EPA	$231.5
VA	$195.0
HHS	$135.7
DHS	$90.7
Export-Import Bank	$90.6
HUD	$65.8
TOP 10 TOTAL	**$7,625.6**
ALL OTHER	**$208.2**
GOVERNMENT TOTAL	**$7,833.8**

SOURCE: TREASURY REPORT ON RECEIVABLES AND DEBT COLLECTION ACTIVITIES
FOURTH QUARTER FY 2008 - 2012

APPENDIX IV: TREASURY OFFSET PROGRAM (TOP) REFERRALS AND COLLECTIONS INCLUDING DEBT OWED TO THE INTERNAL REVENUE SERVICE AND STATE AGENCIES

The Treasury Offset Program (TOP) is the centralized process through which Treasury and other disbursing Federal creditor agencies reduce, or "offset," eligible Federal and State payments, including tax refund payments, to a debtor to satisfy the debtor's past-due Federal non-tax debt and debt owed to State agencies, including child support and unemployment insurance obligations. In addition, the Federal Payment Levy Program, processed through TOP, allows the Internal Revenue Service (IRS) to continuously levy Federal payments due to delinquent Federal taxpayers.[9]

TOP highlights include:

- In FY 2012, $6.0 billion was collected through TOP for Federal and State agencies.
- Past due child support obligations are submitted to TOP by the Department of Health and Human Services (HHS), Office of Child Support Enforcement (OCSE), on behalf of the States and territories.
- As of September 30, 2012, 40 States and the District of Columbia were participating in TOP's State Income Tax Program, whereby Federal tax refunds are offset to collect delinquent State income tax obligations.[10]
- Maryland, New Jersey, New York, Kentucky, Wisconsin, and Minnesota participate in TOP's State Reciprocal Program whereby eligible Federal payments are intercepted to collect debt owed to States, and States intercept State payments to collect delinquent non-tax Federal debt. At least two additional States are expected to join the program in FY 2013, and several others have expressed interest.
- At the end of FY 2012, Federal tax refunds were being offset to collect unemployment compensation debt owed to 18 States and the District of Columbia. Other States continue to join the program.
- Through the tax levy program, $601.6 million of unpaid Federal taxes were collected by TOP.

---

[9] A "levy" is legally distinct from "offset." While offset involves the netting out of mutual obligations between two parties, a levy is a legal seizure of property, usually in the hands of a third party, to satisfy a tax debt.

[10] Nine (9) States do not have an income tax.

FIGURE 28

DEBT REFERRALS TO THE TREASURY OFFSET PROGRAM: FY 2008-2012
(DOLLARS IN BILLIONS)

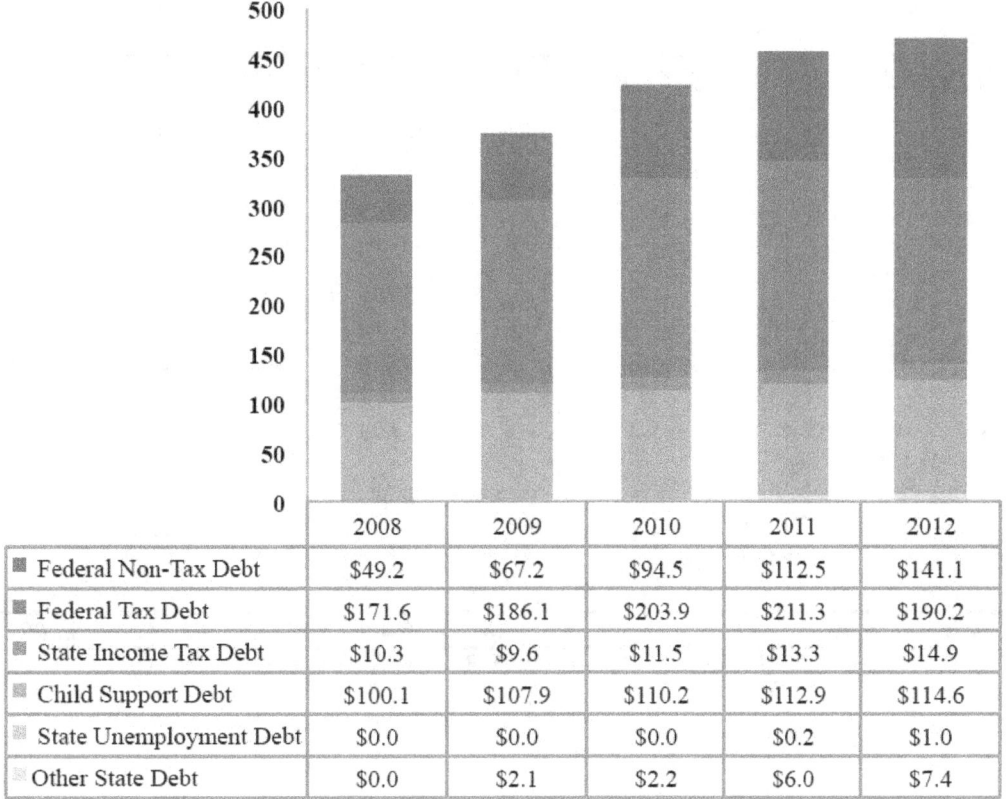

	2008	2009	2010	2011	2012
Federal Non-Tax Debt	$49.2	$67.2	$94.5	$112.5	$141.1
Federal Tax Debt	$171.6	$186.1	$203.9	$211.3	$190.2
State Income Tax Debt	$10.3	$9.6	$11.5	$13.3	$14.9
Child Support Debt	$100.1	$107.9	$110.2	$112.9	$114.6
State Unemployment Debt	$0.0	$0.0	$0.0	$0.2	$1.0
Other State Debt	$0.0	$2.1	$2.2	$6.0	$7.4

SOURCE: DEPARTMENT OF THE TREASURY, BUREAU OF THE FISCAL SERVICE

FIGURE 29

TOP COLLECTION – LEDERAL DEBT: FY 2008-2012
(DOLLARS IN MILLIONS)

TYPE OF DEBT	TYPE OF PAYMENT OFFSET/LEVY	FY 2008	FY 2009	FY 2010	FY 2011	FY 2012
Federal Non-Tax Debt	Tax Refund Offset	$1,948.0	$1,400.0	$1,852.0	$2,180.0	$2,018.9
Federal Non-Tax Debt	Administrative Offset	$221.7	$524.0	$312.8	$426.7	$399.1
Federal Tax Debt	Tax Levy (Federal Payments)	$400.0	$497.0	$617.9	$614.3	$601.6
Total Collected		**$2,569.7**	**$2,421.0**	**$2,782.7**	**$3,221.0**	**$3,019.6**

SOURCE: DEPARTMENT OF THE TREASURY, BUREAU OF THE FISCAL SERVICE

FIGURE 30

TOP COLLECTION – STATE DEBT: FY 2008-2012
(DOLLARS IN MILLIONS)

TYPE OF DEBT	TYPE OF PAYMENT OFFSET	FY 2008	FY 2009	FY 2010	FY 2011	FY 2012
Child Support	Tax Refund Offset	$2,830.0	$2,066.0	$2,086.0	$2,302.0	$2,246.7
State Income Tax Debt	Tax Refund Offset	$358.0	$368.0	$435.1	$475.0	$561.8
State Unemployment Compensation Debt	Tax Refund Offset	N/A	N/A	N/A	$25.9	$132.9
Child Support	Administrative Offset	$4.6	$5.0	$8.3	$10.4	$8.1
State Income Tax Debt (Reciprocal Program)	Administrative Offset	$19.6	$13.0	$9.1	$7.4	$9.2
Other State Debt (Reciprocal Program)	Administrative Offset	$18.6	$12.0	$7.4	$28.8	$44.5
Total Collected		**$3,230.8**	**$2,464.0**	**$2,545.9**	**$2,849.5**	**$3,003.2**

SOURCE: DEPARTMENT OF THE TREASURY, BUREAU OF THE FISCAL SERVICE

APPENDIX V: SOURCES OF DATA

Data contained in this report were obtained from the following sources:

Sources

Treasury Report on Receivables and Debt Collection Activities – Fourth Quarter 2012, as reported by Federal creditor agencies to the Department of the Treasury.

Department of the Treasury, Bureau of the Fiscal Service

Department of Education, Default Resolution Group

Department of Health and Human Services, Program Support Center

Department of Justice, Office of Debt Collection Management

30

www.ingramcontent.com/pod-product-compliance
Lightning Source LLC
Chambersburg PA
CBHW080751290526
45790CB00008B/3411